HAUNTED BALTIMORE

CHARM CITY SPIRITS

To the Spirits who inspire me...

HAUNTED BALTIMORE

ISBN 0-9700718-9-2

Cover design by Sue Miller, Graphic Artist
 Sheridan Books, Ann Arbor, MI

Cover photo by author.

Logo design by Glenda Moore, catStuff Graphics.

Printed on recycled paper by Sheridan Books,
Fredericksburg, VA.

CONTENTS

INTRODUCTION

Ghosts have permeated the human psyche for millennia and remain one of life's great mysteries. They seem to live an active afterlife and every once in a while when they drop into our dimension, quite by accident, their presence is startling.

Many consider them menacing, no doubt due to media representation, but in truth they are benign beings caught between worlds trying to work out the issues that keep them earthbound.

We can surmise that some of the spiritual residue of the Charm City's long dead citizens is leftover energy triggered by some emotional event that has resulted in mystifying phenomena.

Birthplace of the famous Baltimore clipper ships, the ghosts stationed aboard the *USS Constellation* feel right at home moored in the Inner Harbor. Not everyone believes that ghosts exist on this ship but credible sources provided an ethereal photograph and eyewitness testimony as evidence to support the spirits' presence on the revered vessel.

Charming Fells Point, the nation's oldest surviving maritime community, exudes an Old English atmosphere with its quaint shops, plentiful pubs, and awesome ghosts. A staunch belief in the afterlife is a British tradition that may be a factor in the large number of ghosts that populate the tiny community.

The ancient neighborhood's "brothels, bars, and boarding houses," to borrow the Preservation Society's phrase, gave birth to a plethora of spirits whose energy is embedded in the cobblestone streets.

Known for its luscious seafood, dining at one of Balto's haunted restaurants and downing a pint or two is a must for all those who hunger and thirst for ghosts.

Edgar Allan Poe called Baltimore home for a while and died here on his way to New York. His mortal remains rest in Westminster Hall's spooky cemetery just around the corner from his former home, widely held to be haunted. The dark poet's spirit also broods in a Fells Point bar.

Baltimore's Museum of Industry is housed in a 19th century cannery; learn about the region's industrial heritage via the museum's fascinating hands-on exhibits and realistic renderings of life during that era. Maybe you'll discern the variety of specters also on display, albeit in another dimension.

Every year thousands visit our national shrine, historic Fort McHenry, birthplace of the *Star Spangled Banner*. Those who witnessed the fort's paranormal phenomena contend that the Battle of Baltimore is still being waged in the spirit world. Some spirits stay behind out of a sense of duty, which may be the case at the ancient fort.

Perhaps dedication is why the spirit of devoted librarian, Marcia Noyes, lingers at the Medical and Chirurgical Library as well.

Not all of Baltimore's economic successes were by sea. By 1874, Robert Garrett's Baltimore & Ohio Railroad stretched to Chicago. Ten years later his home in Mount Vernon was "the finest mansion Baltimore had ever seen." Mrs. Garrett's soirées were legendary; the high energy generated by the jovial occasions is imprinted on the place and phantom partygoers still find the grand house to their liking.

Some spirits are just confused and don't realize they're dead. Several years ago, Club Charles' "Frenchie" the ghost and the Zodiac Restaurant's "linen-clad man" were presented on the History Channel; their beguiling stories a Baltimore favorite.

These are just a sampling of the true ghost stories presented in *Haunted Baltimore*. Read on and discover there is more to this charming city than meets the eye.

(Photo by Author)

Awesome ghosts are stationed aboard the
USS CONSTELLATION.

USS CONSTELLATION

After a long and distinguished career, the USS Constellation, the last Civil War-era vessel still afloat, makes its home in Baltimore's Inner Harbor.

Considered one of our nation's treasures, the stalwart frigate saw action in five wars, from 1854 up until World War II. While touring this fully restored craft, which helped to curtail the slave trade and transported food to famine victims in Ireland, keep a lookout for apparitions.

In 1955, when the historic ship was moored near the submarine *Pike*, the sub's crew observed phantoms walking along the *Constellation*'s decks and heard the usual noises associated with sailors going about their seafaring duties.

Lieutenant Commander Allen Ross Brougham captured one of the sea-going apparitions on film. The photo showed a bluish-white figure dressed in an old-fashioned uniform and wearing a sword. The amazing photo, published in the *Baltimore Sun*, clearly showed a nebulous form on deck.

Is this Naval ghost the soul image of someone who may have lost his life while in service to his country? Perhaps it was yeoman Neil Harvey.

Harvey served on the frigate *USF Constellation* that was launched in Baltimore in 1797. The ill-fated yeoman made the unpardonable mistake of falling asleep on his watch and there was hell to pay.

The hateful skipper, Captain Truxton, wanted to teach his crew a lesson and make sure that no other sailor would ever doze off while on duty. He ordered Harvey bound to a cannon. The great gun was ignited and the sailor was blown to bits.

Harvey feels right at home aboard the newer *Constellation* — often his specter is mistaken for a costumed re-enactor.

Sensitive types may also discern the foreboding presence of the evil Captain still ruling the roost.

Another ghost stationed on the Navy's last all-sail ship is a night watchman who dares not rest in peace as long as the mean-spirited Captain Truxton remains on board; he stays awake by merrily playing cards below the deck.

The ship's haunted history records the story of a priest who went on board and was shown around the vessel by a man who exhibited great knowledge of the ship. The reverend later discovered that no such person worked there as a guide.

It's widely held that the night watchman, so familiar with the ship's recesses, provides tours that are literally out of this world.

FELLS POINT

Listed on the National Register of Historic Districts, Fells Point boasts many houses and commercial buildings dating from the 18th and 19th centuries.

The town's history began in 1730, when William Fell, an immigrant from Lancashire, England purchased a 100 acre tract called Copus Harbor; he built a home and a small shipyard where he planned to construct double-masted sailing vessels.

In 1773, William's son Edward subdivided the family's real estate holdings into a town he called Fells Point. He chose English names for the streets, such as Thames and Shakespeare, and pleasant names for the alleys - Apple, Happy, Petticoat. Fell then sold the parcels to speculators eager to cash in on the deepwater port's potential and its close proximity to iron foundries and timber.

Fells Point rapidly became a shipbuilding center; the area produced many of the ships and sailors that led America to victory during the Revolution. Ship owners and captains built the 2½ story dormered homes that exist today; offices took up the first floor, the upper floor served as the family living area, and children and servants lived in the attic.

The Fell family gravestone is a silent tribute to the visionaries that changed the course of Baltimore's history. When all is quiet on Shakespeare Street, furtive apparitions of the male members of the Fell family make their presence known.

By the War of 1812, Baltimore's clipper ships, renowned for their speed, dominated the high seas.

Unfortunately, an economic depression followed the conflict and commerce crawled to a halt. In 1832, a yellow fever epidemic decimated the population. These downturns certainly account for some of the spirits still in residence.

Residential Fells Point ultimately deteriorated and many original dwellings were razed for industrial expansion. The lowest point in the neighborhood's 250-year history came when plans were made for an expressway along the waterfront. Local citizens rallied to save the neighborhood and by 1967 successfully thwarted the extension of Route 95.

The Preservation Society of Fells Point helped save the vicinity from the highway and preserved what was left of the city's heritage.

Today dozens of the 350 original 18th century residential structures have been restored. (It's no wonder that the long dead feel right at home here.) Residents, shopkeepers, bar and restaurant owners are well aware of the specters that unobtrusively pervade their space.

In the 1970's a man bought one of the historic buildings sadly in need of extensive renovation. He looked forward to uncovering some long ago treasure and, after a while, began his search in the attic.

At the top of the narrow stairway, he unbolted the door, obviously secured for many, many years. Entering the diminutive room he found old furniture and children's belongings dusted with cobwebs. Under an ancient blanket that fell to pieces upon his touch, he discovered a skeleton in the small bed.[1]

After that, he began to hear a child crying at night. He sold the place a year later.

Another homeowner wanted to replace the floorboards and ripped up the old ones exposing a pair of skeletons lying side by side - one wore a crumbling dress the other donned disintegrating male attire.

Having disturbed their resting place, the family claimed they heard eerie scratching under the floorboards,[2] a chilling incident reminiscent of an Edgar Allan Poe horror story.

When all is quiet in the tiny town all types of ghosts parade the alleyways and storied streets.

Reliable citizens have witnessed apparitions of Revolutionary War types, still intent on the cause. Even the spirits of William and Edward Fell dressed in their 18th century best still walk the streets the family so carefully laid out. Furtive shades duck down alleys dissolving before baffled observers catch another glimpse.

---

[1] John Kurluk, "Ghosts of Fells Point."
[2] Ibid.

Near Thames and Bond Streets some people have strained to hear distant voices faintly murmuring. Others have heard men on ships preparing to dock or launch. A lone woman called the "lady of the misty nights" walks along the waterfront...

Given Fells Point's history, and what remains of its glory days, ghostly residents are plentiful and add a spooky flair to its rich heritage. They are as genuine and as unique as the town's real-life inhabitants.

(Photo: Robbin Van Pelt)

Fells Point is full of history and haunted places.

(Photo: Robbin Van Pelt)

Who's looking out for Baltimore?

THE SENTRY
501-503 South Eastern Avenue

The imposing commercial building at the corner of Broadway and Eastern Avenue was put up as a department store by prominent retailers, B. Noah & Sons, in 1898. This is the family's second edifice on that site.

Some say that today the structure's tower harbors a leftover spirit from Revolutionary War days.

Late at night passersby have observed the tower's uppermost windows aglow with a pale yellow light. Looking closer they discern a tall figure holding a lantern. He moves slowly around the confined space and intently peers out each window.

The story goes that the pigtailed sentry is looking out for the enemy, perhaps British warships on voyage to Fort McHenry.

When he's completed his rounds the light goes out until his next appointed watch.

Others familiar with the building say that objects forever go missing inside the massive space.

LANCASTER STREET

There once was an old woman known as Aunt Julia who lived in a certain house on Lancaster Street her entire life. When Julia died, a man purchased the house fully furnished.

One night he carelessly perched on a rickety stool he found inside the house and attempted to repair a crack in the plaster. As the stool began to tip, he felt two strong hands on the back of his legs holding him upright even though he was alone in the house.

Her nieces and nephews recalled that almost on a daily basis, Aunt Julia had warned them never to use the unwieldy stool.

Julia paid the children with a shiny new penny for each room they cleaned. Now, whenever a resident straightens a room, they always find a shiny penny lying in the middle of the floor.

BERTHA'S MUSSELS
734 South Broadway

Bertha's is a Fells Point landmark and home to the famous "Eat Bertha's Mussels" bumper stickers spotted all over the world advertising the succulent shellfish.

Established in 1972, owners Laura and Tony Norris christened the business "Bertha's" when they were inspired by a name found on a stained glass window they acquired from a church that was being remodeled.

Bertha's is also noteworthy for the ghosts who reside inside the aged structure that once operated as a brothel.

In 1832 a yellow fever epidemic swept through Fells Point and claimed innumerable lives. Some feel the apparition of a little girl dressed in Victorian clothing may be a victim of the awful plague. When observed she is described as looking lonely and sad and exudes a yearning feeling. Her startling appearances aren't frightening, but nevertheless employees feel uncomfortable in her presence.

Ghosts linger because they're confused and don't realize they're dead. No doubt, this poor waif is caught between worlds and longs to be reunited with her family.

Another specter spotted on occasion is a woman in black - another puzzled phantom seeking peace yet still attached to the mortal world for reasons we can only ponder...

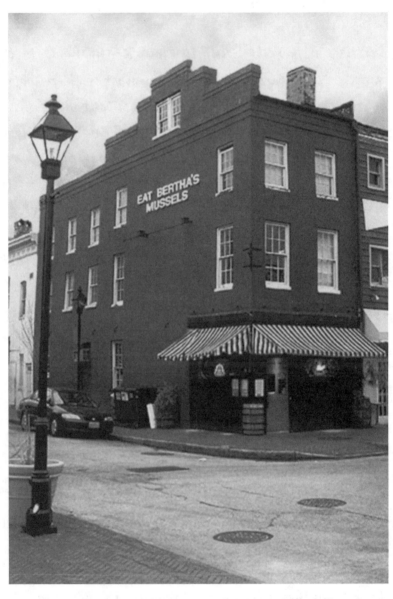

(Photo: Robbin Van Pelt)

Bertha's Mussels

One more ghost who enjoys the ambiance of the shabby chic restaurant is a pipe-smoking patron. A female diner inquired if the eatery was haunted because she had observed an old man sitting alone at a nearby table smoking a pipe; when a waiter passed by the old guy's table the diner looked over and the old man was gone.

Many times spirits seem to hover on stairwells. Maryland ghost hunters have captured on film what appears to be ectoplasm on the stairs leading to the second floor. Often staff and bar patrons on the ground floor hear banging noises, footsteps, and partying overhead. No living soul is ever found and even though the second floor is wired with a motion detector the alarm is never tripped.

Bertha's benign spirits peacefully co-exist with the living.

EAT BERTHA'S
MUSSELS

FRIENDS
1634 Aliceanna Street

Friends is the only Fells Point establishment that operated as a bar, restaurant, hotel, and brothel. Constructed in 1876, the place has a lively past that has spawned a variety of specters.

Old salts reminisce about the days as Dix's Hotel and long ago bar fights; stabbing victims got stitched up on the spot. These belligerent brawls may account for the "shadow people" observed upstairs.

The back room, now the billiards room, was once a family living area. On occasion, an old woman in a rocking chair still inhabits this vintage space.

A man employed by a former owner was sleeping upstairs when he felt as though he was being strangled. He later learned that a fellow had hung himself up there in the 1940s. Manager Ben Naas shared that upon entering this room on a warm summer day, the temperature instantly dropped to freezing.

Photos taken at this colorful nightspot reveal orbs of light floating about the building and unaccountable white streaks suspected to be ghostly ectoplasm.

One night at closing a server saw an older gentleman sitting at the bar with a beer in front of him. She was about to speak to him, reconsidered, and when she turned back he was gone.

THE WHARF RAT
801 South Anne Street

This old seaman's tavern, filled with authentic seafaring décor and glass coasters salvaged from long defunct breweries, has operated as a tavern since it opened in the 1790s. Edgar Allen Poe downed his fair share here and the tavern was the first bar to be licensed in Baltimore after prohibition.

A fellow named Harry Thompson owned the place in the early thirties. He had a brother Thomas who worked for him and lived upstairs. He also had a son Dougie who worked as a bartender and loved loud music. Being an old building, the noise carried.

Old Thomas complained about the blaring music but it didn't do any good. One night the noise was too much to bear. He came downstairs after Dougie who refused to turn down the volume - old Tom shot Dougie dead right on the spot.

This story was told to owner Bill Oliver by Miss Eleanor, a life time resident of Fells Point, now in her nineties. She was just a young girl at the time and still comes in for a glass of Baileys every once in a while.

Now that the Olivers operate the pub, there's a strange occurrence from time to time.

"During a busy night when the place is rocking, the music will suddenly, inexplicably drop in volume. We had a tape player and this happened, we replaced it with a CD player, same thing. We put in a jukebox, still the same. We even started to subscribe to a cable music system. We called in B.G.E. to evaluate our power supply. We've had several different electrical companies pour over our place. When "Homicide" the T.V. series filmed at the Wharf Rat we had the professional sound men try to explain this phenomenon. No one can give us an answer. When the music gets too loud, why does it suddenly drop in volume?"

According to Miss Eleanor, it's the ghost of Old Tommy Thompson. There has been one other person shot at this pub but that's another story...

(Photo: Robbin Van Pelt)

(Photo: Robbin Van Pelt)

Ed Kane's Water Taxi can transport you to an array of Balto's haunted places. When purchasing your ticket at the old Merchants House, 1732 Thames Street, inquire about "Penelope;" her ghostly visage is sometimes seen peering out the window.

The Cat's Eye Pub

THE CAT'S EYE PUB
1730 Thames Street

The haunting sounds of the world's oldest profession are still alive and clicking at The Cat's Eye Pub where the ladies of the evening are still working the well-worn cobbled streets of old Baltimore.

Fells Point was a thriving port for over 100 years and attracted all sorts of characters who frequented the brothels that flourished in the harbor town. Originally shaped like a hook, the peninsula was inhabited by "ladies of the night" looking to get by. Historians suggest the term "hooker" derives from this state of affairs.

During renovation, workman found numerous red light switches on the walls. These light switches were a common necessity in brothels - when a woman was occupied, her red light bulb would be off - if she were available for "services," her red light would be on. Hence, the term, "red light district."

According to some pub patrons several ladies of the evening are still in residence at the Cat's Eye. Although the notorious light switches are now hidden under dry wall and paint, the unmistakable clicking of the switches can still be heard.

The Whistling Oyster

THE WHISTLING OYSTER
807 South Broadway

Broadway is the main thoroughfare through Fells Point and like many of the taverns and shops in the colorful neighborhood, the Whistling Oyster operates from the ground floor of a rowhouse.

The bar was featured on *America's Most Haunted Places*. An actor portrayed the apparition of the African American dressed in Colonial garb often seen sweeping and cleaning up after hours. To the consternation of the owner the faithful phantom kept a careful eye on an ash bucket and moved it from room to room.

Another wraith inside The Whistling Oyster is a shadowy figure ascending a staircase that no longer exists. Workers and patrons alike have clearly heard the sound of his disembodied footsteps running up and down the flight of stairs that accompany his eternal climb.

(Photo: Robbin Van Pelt)

Leadbetters Tavern

LEADBETTERS TAVERN
1639 Thames Street

Leadbetters Tavern opened in the 1960's and was named after Huddie (William) Ledbetter, also known as "Leadbelly."

Leadbelly (1888-1949) was an American blues singer with a violent streak; he was incarcerated for most of his life and on two occasions sang himself out of his jail sentence. Leadbelly's music was the spark that triggered the folk and blues revivals of the 1950s and 60s.

The singer was born near Shreveport, Louisiana but grew up in Texas; his father was a musician and taught him accordion.

In 1916, Leadbelly was jailed for assault but managed to break away from the chain gang. He evaded the authorities by using an alias but was apprehended when he shot and killed a man in an argument over a woman.

While serving a 30-year sentence he composed a song that begged Texas governor Pat Neff for a pardon. He was released. Five years later he was back behind bars at Louisiana's State Penitentiary. Leadbelly reworked the song that had influenced Governor Neff, and in 1934 Governor O.K. Allen shortened his sentence.

Folklorists sought out the singer to record his music for posterity for the Library of Congress. They took

Ledbetter to New York, and published a book about him in 1936. While in Manhattan, Leadbelly recorded his best-known songs, *The Rock Island Line*, *Midnight Special*, and *Goodnight Irene*.

A few years later Leadbelly was once again singing the blues in the slammer on Riker's Island this time for assault during a drunken brawl.

During the 1940s Leadbelly's home in New York was a gathering place for folk and blues singers such as Brownie McGhee and Woody Guthrie.

After he died in 1949, The Weavers folk group recorded *Goodnight Irene* and it rocketed to the top of the pop charts. In 1976, Gordon Parks produced the film *Leadbelly*, based on the singer's life. [3]

When local ghost hunters investigated the tavern for possible paranormal activity, they captured on film a white, streaky figure, certain they had photographed Leadbelly's ghostly presence.

Maybe he has sung his way out of his grave and is now locked up in his namesake tavern making up for time lost behind bars.

Most likely, however, the ectoplasm is the spirit of a young, dark haired man in a white ruffled shirt who appears in the bar from time to time. History records the murder of a sailor in the back alley so perhaps this ghost is just picking up where fate so suddenly cut him off.

---

[3] www.leadbetterstavern.com

DUDA'S TAVERN
1600 Thames Street

When the newly hired bartender ventured into Duda's basement, she observed a man with curly black hair dressed in white trousers and a vintage navy blue sailor top; she did a double take and the man was gone.

The proprietor was not surprised to hear of the encounter because ghosts are everywhere in the three-story rowhouse.

In the 1850s the structure was put up as the Union Hotel. Thirty years later it hailed as the headquarters for the Maryland Bay Pilots Association, then it became a seamen's rooming house complete with a chapel. When Prohibition ended, a tavern was established on the first floor.

The Dudas have owned the place since 1949 and sightings of mysterious wraiths of all descriptions are commonplace, their presence usually accompanied by an ice-cold breeze.

Once when an electrician was upgrading the wiring system, he spotted an older man in a flannel shirt. The electrician tried to strike up a conversation with the dude but the intruder faded from his sight.

The workman fled the building and locked himself in his truck; co-workers finally managed to coax him back to work.

(Photo: Robbin Van Pelt)

Duda's

As a joke, a bartender quietly entered the basement and tapped the electrician on his shoulder; the poor guy jerked as if jolted by an electric shock, banged his head on the ceiling, and ran from the place never to pass through its portals again.

After closing, when the din of the crowds have subsided, workers cleaning up for the night have heard footsteps and chairs being pulled across the floors overhead. When they investigate, all they find is an empty room.

Could this be "Doc" living out an otherworldly existence? Doc was a merchant seaman who lived upstairs for decades. His favorite song on the jukebox was a quirky polka - Doc was the only one who would ever play it.

One evening, months after the seaman passed away in 1980, the bar filled with strains of Doc's polka, yet hadn't the awful record been removed from the jukebox...? When the jukebox was unlocked, management discovered that the record was nowhere to be found!

(Photo: Robbin Van Pelt)

The Horse You Came In On

THE HORSE YOU CAME IN ON
1626 Thames Street

Fells Point was a favored haunt of Edgar Allan Poe when he lived in Baltimore. He cut a dashing figure about the bawdy town in his sweeping black cape.

Poe's favorite watering hole stood where The Horse You Came In On now stands. On the night he died they found the brooding poet laying facedown in a gutter on Lombard Street; he was on his way home from the pub when he passed out.

In recent years, two barkeeps were horsing around and mocked Poe's decadent lifestyle and made fun of the way the poet strode about the city in his signature cape. No sooner were the words out of their mouths than a dozen barstools tottered across the room and banged against the wall.

To pacify the disturbed spirit, the guilty men poured a shot of single-malt whisky and left it on the bar. The practice continues at closing to this day. Patrons can order the drink "whisky - single-malt, no ice" - they call it "the Edgar."

Psychics intuit that Poe's spirit inhabits the pub and attribute the strange occurrences throughout the bar to the long-gone writer.

"The tavern's chandeliers swing all by themselves," recounted a bartender, then she offered an eerie memory.

One morning as she passed the cash register, the money drawer opened. She closed the drawer and went about her business. To her surprise, the drawer opened again. This tug-o'-war with the till continued until the bar opened for business that day.

At the end of her shift she told the night bartender about the incident. Amazingly he had experienced the same thing several times in the past.

The employees are fond of "Edgar" and often commune with his spirit. It's usually around closing that the eeriness occurs and all present are certain to acknowledge the unseen presence and pour him a drink. – whoever it is.

EDGAR ALLAN POE HOUSE

Born in 1809, Edgar Allan Poe is best known for his dark poetry and macabre stories such as "The Telltale Heart," "The Pit and the Pendulum," and "The Fall of the House of Usher."

Poe called himself a "Virginia gentleman," although he considered Baltimore his home. Born of actor parents while they were on tour in Boston, Poe claimed Baltimore as his birthplace.

When he was 18 years old, Poe enlisted in the Army and while attending West Point, decided that Army life was not for him. He returned to Baltimore and worked to support himself while he continued writing.

He lived in a small five-room house at 203 Amity Street with his aunt, Maria, and her daughter, Virginia, whom he later married. His first success was "MS found in a Bottle" for which he won first prize - $50. In the tiny attic room he penned eleven stories, eight poems, and several reviews and editorials while in residence on Amity Street from 1833 to 1835.

In 1941, the Edgar Allan Poe Society of Baltimore saved the 19th century house from demolition. The national historic landmark stands next to Edgar Allan Poe Homes, the first public housing project in Baltimore.

(Photo by Author)

Edgar Allan Poe House and Museum

Locals say the spirit of "Mr. Eddie" watches over the house and nearby neighborhood.

Some of the paranormal phenomena reported are that visitors feel phantom taps on their shoulder and cold spots, doors and windows open on their own, voices murmur, and lights flicker.

Years ago locals reported that the lights were on all night in the house even though the power was out throughout the neighborhood.

Some have even reported seeing a female ghost in the house. Could it be Maria Clemm? They describe the apparition as a heavyset woman in a 19th century style gray dress.

"There are some secrets that do not permit themselves to be revealed."

~ Edgar Allan Poe

ORIGINAL BURIAL PLACE OF
EDGAR ALLAN POE
FROM
OCTOBER 9, 1849,
UNTIL
NOVEMBER 17, 1875.

MRS. MARIA CLEMM HIS MOTHER-IN-LAW,
AND VIRGINIA POE
HIS WIFE WHO ARE LEFT UNDER THE
MONUMENT ERECTED TO HIM IN THIS
CEMETERY.

(Photo by Author)

Edgar Allan Poe's Grave

WESTMINSTER BURYING GROUND

Close by Edgar Allan Poe's Amity Street abode is Westminster Hall's ancient graveyard and the poet's infamous burial plot.

The Presbyterian Church at Fayette and Green Streets was built over part of the cemetery and many of the graves can only be reached via the catacombs. Rumors of restless spirits roaming the burial chambers abound, particularly that of a little girl, yet a mysterious visitor to the cemetery every January 19th eclipses their presence.

Poe was originally interred in an unmarked grave but when the neglected site was criticized, his cousin ordered a headstone. Before the marker could be installed, a train derailed and crashed into the monument yard destroying the headstone.

Five years later, Sara Sigourney Rice, a Baltimore schoolteacher, began a campaign to raise money for a fitting monument to honor the forsaken poet. Students donated their "pennies for Poe," friends and benefactors made up the balance.

Dedicated on November 17, 1875, Walt Whitman attended, and commemorative letters from Henry Wadsworth Longfellow, John Greenleaf Whittier,

William Cullen Bryant, and Alfred Lord Tennyson were read.

Virginia Poe's remains were re-interred from New York and in 1885, when his aunt Maria Clemm died the family was finally reunited in the burial ground.

Westminster Hall was featured on TV's *Sightings*. Many of the graves at this church date to the 1700's and ghost-hunters have a field day here with their electronic magnetic field detectors. They have also successfully audio taped ghostly mutterings from beyond the grave.

Traditionally, visitors place coins on Poe's headstone. One writer suggested leaving some dry cat food for the many felines that keep vigil over the graveyard. One in particular favors Poe's resting spot - a spry black cat enjoys sunning himself on the macabre author's grave.

Since 1949, a mysterious stranger makes a yearly pilgrimage to Poe's grave and leaves behind three red roses and a partial bottle of French cognac. It is surmised that the three roses represent Poe, his wife, and beloved aunt.

The strange man, dubbed the "phantom," dons a black hat, black overcoat and white scarf and shows up between midnight and dawn every January 19th to toast the author on his birthday. No one knows his identity but it is believed that the anonymous man's son has taken up the ritual.

Edgar Allan Poe monument in Westminster Hall
burying ground.

MUSEUM OF INDUSTRY

When sailing gave way to steamships, Baltimore's wharves were too small for the large vessels and the shipyards were forced to close. Canning and packaging and lumber companies quickly took over and the area became industrialized.

Baltimore's Museum of Industry, at 1415 Key Highway, was founded in 1977 to preserve the city's industrial heritage (just as the canning industry was founded to preserve the riches of the Chesapeake Bay when shipped, for the first time, to other parts of the country).

Witnesses to the odd goings on in the historic Platt Oyster Cannery building (c.1865) are "credible sources," intelligent, trustworthy, and convinced that the museum is haunted.

A former archivist emerged from the machine shop one day and stated that a power saw had suddenly started to run. When the worker went to turn it off, the machine wasn't even plugged in!

Another worker stored some heavy cartons in a particular place before closing up shop; the next morning he found them moved across the room. There was no explanation.

On several occasions a museum tour guide saw a man wearing dated clothing walk right through a sealed door in the museum's print gallery.

Work stalls located in the basement, which is off limits to the public, were likely used by immigrants or African Americans kept separate from the other workers by segregation policies enforced in the 19th century.[1] These employees were also paid less and were expected to produce more. Perhaps their spirits stay behind to right wrongful attitudes.

The apparitions could be victims of abuse or accidents suffered at the site. That might explain the cries that pierce the late night air.

Other anomalies are giggling sounds in the kid's cannery, the printing press runs when nobody's around, the sound of a hammer striking an anvil resonates, and slow, high-pitched singing emanates from what was once the public relations office.

Staffers are dedicated to preserving the relics of Baltimore's past and treat their spirits with the same consideration. They too are part and parcel of a rich heritage – although haunted.

[1] Rob Williams, "Things That Go Bump in the Museum,"

Many ancient forts bear the supernatural imprints of violent battles, but Fort McHenry is unique in that it is the only site in the National Park System that is designated as both a national monument and a historic shrine.

(National Park Service photos.)

Forevermore, the star-spangled banner waves proudly over haunted Fort McHenry.

FORT McHENRY

Fort McHenry is Baltimore's most popular tourist destination. Birthplace of our national anthem, since 1933, the National Park Service has administered the very historic, and *haunted*, bastion.

Our story begins in 1812... by this time Fells Point shipyards had perfected the Baltimore Clipper; the ships' speed and maneuverability had enabled the capture of over 500 British ships by Baltimore based privateers. Hundreds of thousands of dollars of cargo was seized igniting hostilities on September 13, 1814.

Although greatly outnumbered and ill equipped, American forces staved off fierce British attacks by land and sea.

Lieutenant Levi Clagett, along with several of his men, was killed instantly when a British warship bombarded the bastion during the assault that inspired the "Star-Spangled Banner."

Built between 1794 and 1803, Fort McHenry's five-pointed star design is based on a French pattern popular during the reign of Louis XIV (1643-1715).

Bastion three, one of the star-shaped fort's five points, is called "Clagett's Bastion."

There are those who feel Clagett's spirit lives on at the fort. Often mistaken for a re-enactor, several visitors have reported seeing Clagett's ghost dressed in a uniform unique to that era.

On the same day, but at different times, two park rangers observed a man's shadow on a wall near the spot where Clagett was gunned down nearly two centuries ago. They independently investigated the source of the shade but could find no source for the strange silhouette or the disembodied footsteps accompanying the phenomenon.

Unofficially, park rangers are baffled by windows that open and close of their own accord, sounds of slamming doors, and lights found on when they're certain they'd been turned off.

Another specter still on duty at the historic stronghold is Private John Drew. The 28 year-old, who hailed from Virginia, was ordered to stand guard on the night of November 14, 1880. The next morning his relief found Drew asleep at his post.

Drew was immediately arrested and taken to the guardhouse where he secreted a rifle into his cell. When left alone, the mortified soldier stuck the muzzle into his mouth and pulled the trigger.

A ranger's dog may have had an otherworldly encounter with Private Drew. One evening as the canine explored the seawall he came to the spot on the battery where Drew was caught snoozing. The dog seemed to sense an invisible presence, snarled and cowered, and finally scampered back to the safety of his owner.

Could it be that Private Drew's spirit stays on guard at old Fort McHenry to atone for his lapse when alive?

During the Civil War Confederate prisoners were held captive in the citadel's dungeons.

One young man related that in 1998, he and his friends were at the fort exploring the dungeons. At closing time, they headed out but stopped in their tracks when they heard indistinguishable voices along with loud noises that sounded as if someone was dropping a heavy load on the stone floor.

As they cautiously approached the noise, their blood ran cold when they spied two men, dressed in drab old clothes from an earlier day, dropping barrels of ammunition on the floor. The bloodied apparitions seemed oblivious to the awestruck boys.

When the ghosts finished their job, they turned and disappeared through the wall. Immediately, a small contingent of men followed who also exited through the walls.

After the Battle of Baltimore, Fort McHenry never again came under siege, although it remained a (spiritually) active military post off and on for the next hundred years.

FRANCIS SCOTT KEY HOUSE

When Francis Scott Key caught sight of the American flag still aloft over Fort McHenry after the Battle of Baltimore, he was inspired to immortalize the victory in a poem that later became our national anthem.

Forever linked to Baltimore, Francis Scott Key was a respected young lawyer living in Georgetown just west of the modern day Key Bridge. House proud, the attorney was meticulous about his property.

After much wrangling to preserve his domicile, the forsaken house was torn down in 1947 to make way for an access road. Rumor has it that the planners named the bridge after Key to allay his angry spirit.[2]

It bears telling that after the attorney died in 1843, "sinister sounds" filled his deteriorating home on M Street. Most likely the creaking, squeaks, and moans were Key's technique to persuade tenants to restore the house to its former glory.

---

[2] John Alexander, *Ghosts, Washington's Most Famous Ghost Stories.*

GARRETT-JACOBS MANSION

In the heart of Baltimore's Mount Vernon district a statue of George Washington surveys the city from atop a towering marble monument erected in his honor in 1829.

During the 19th century the area was forested and known as "Howard's Woods" a popular destination on patriotic holidays.

Ultimately, four parks were laid out and soon the squares were filled with Baltimore's finest residences. Today the area is home to nearly a dozen cultural institutions.

In 1884, the president of the B&O Railroad, Robert Garrett, commissioned Stanford White to build "the finest mansion Baltimore had ever seen."

The renowned architect outdid himself. Number 11 West Mount Vernon Place is a grand townhouse containing 40 rooms, 100 windows and 16 fireplaces. It housed a theater, art gallery and a conservatory. The centerpiece of the dwelling is the three-story staircase adorned by Tiffany glass windows.

Mrs. Garrett, the former Mary Sloane Frick, and later Mrs. Henry Barton Jacobs, was the style guru of

Baltimore society. Her elegant parties were legendary - her entertainment skills unequaled. She passed away in 1936.

A horrific fire decimated Baltimore in 1904 and the Engineers Club was established to redesign the city. In 1961, the society purchased the Garret-Jacobs Mansion.

Recent staffers allege that shadows often pass down the second-floor corridor. A velvet rope that cordons off a restricted area in the basement swings as if moved by unseen hands.

According to an article in the *Baltimore Sun*, Peter Weston was at one time the society's food and beverage director. One morning, Weston passed through the room that used to be the Garretts' dining room. The director stopped dead in his tracks when he discerned a group of jovial diners at the table enjoying an elaborate meal. A passing co-worker remarked that Weston looked like he had just seen a ghost. Indeed he had - several of them. The phantom party simply faded away.

On another occasion, the Women's Auxiliary had a heavy piece of sculpture moved from the library window to a Tiffany window near the stairs. At the end of the day, the director locked up and set the alarm.

The next morning the sculpture was back in its original niche. The only person who could have moved it was an elderly handyman, Manny Burse. When confronted, Burse denied the allegation and insisted he hadn't touched the sculpture.

Several years later, the handyman tendered his resignation on Christmas Eve, to take effect New Year's Day. Burse became ill and died on New Year's Eve. He never had the opportunity to enjoy his retirement.

Months later the director saw Burse sitting in a chair by the main bar where he always took his morning break. Weston said "hi" without any thought and then it hit him (along with a chill down his spine). When Weston looked back, the chair was empty.

(National Park Service Photo)

The spirit of a devoted librarian stays amid the stacks at the Medical and Chirurgical Library.

MEDICAL AND CHIRURGICAL LIBRARY

Baltimore's Medical and Chirurgical Faculty Library was established in 1830; it was the second state medical society library founded in the United States and is the oldest such library still in operation.[3]

The library assists physicians' research and houses the history of medicine.

For fifty years, Marcia Crocker Noyes served as librarian. Her appointment in 1896 at the age of twenty-seven was groundbreaking because this was the first time a non-physician held the post and she was the first woman to head the library.

Dr. William Osler, a professor at Johns Hopkins School of Medicine, was disappointed with the small, disorganized, and outdated library, and decided that an "intelligent and dedicated" full-time librarian was needed. Recommended for the position by her employer at the Enoch Pratt Free Library, Noyes modestly proclaimed her only qualification for the position was that she was able to reside in the library and be on-call 24 hours a day.

The New York native, a graduate of Hunter College,

---

[3] Joseph E. Jensen & Ingreet Weisheit-Smith, "History of the Library of the Medical and Chirurgical Faculty of the State of Maryland."

readily admitted she had no medical background but immediately set about gaining the necessary knowledge.

Initially the physicians had reservations regarding a young, single female librarian, some were downright hostile, but Noyes attended every faculty function and stayed current on all activities.

Her proudest accomplishment was the present building constructed in 1909 at 1211 Academy Street. For an entire year she constantly raised funds and oversaw every structural detail. Her new lodgings were on the fourth floor and she referred to them as Baltimore's first penthouse.

Her small staff stayed extremely loyal because she always gave them the credit when things went right and always took the blame when things went wrong.

Under Noyes' leadership the library grew to 65,000 volumes. She developed her own book classification system and helped found the Medical Library Association to which she was elected president in 1934. Another pioneering feat, for she was the first woman and non-physician elected, attesting to the respect she engendered.

Over 250 physicians attended Noyes' fiftieth anniversary reception in 1946. Due to her failing health, the party was held in April, six months early. As it turns out she died on November 24th, fifty years to the date of her hire.

According to her wishes, Marcia's funeral was held in the library's auditorium; sixty doctors served as honorary pallbearers.

After her death, the Medical Library Association initiated the Marcia C. Noyes Award to recognize outstanding achievement in medical librarianship.

Characteristically, Marcia Noyes' spirit goes about its work at Med Chi, albeit in another dimension. Reportedly the librarian gently haunts all four floors.

When all is still and quiet in the book repository, and workers are alone, footsteps on the cast-iron stairs, the sound of books being placed on shelves, and book trucks being wheeled through the stacks are audible.

On the beautiful, winding, marble stairway, disembodied footsteps going up and down and followed or preceded by the sound of a door opening and closing is a common phenomena.[4]

Amazingly, just hours before this book went to press, the first known sighting of Marcia's apparition occurred in the auditorium.

Long-time employee Leatha Hardy saw a woman dressed in black working at the podium. The worker called out "hello" but the woman was oblivious; Leatha watched until the woman walked away. Later, when shown Marcia's photo, Leatha affirmed that indeed this was the person she had seen.

---

[4] Joseph E. Jensen, "Med-Chi's Diligent Ghost."

(Photo: Robbin Van Pelt)

A phantom piano player tickles the ivories at Baltimore's Theater Project.

THEATER PROJECT

The Theater Project is a landmark in Baltimore's Cultural District and noted for its avant-garde performances.

A fraternal organization known as the Improved Order of Heptasophs erected the building at 45 W. Preston Street in 1883. In the 1920s and '30s the structure operated as a dance hall.

For years, stories of a phantom piano player have plagued the place. The spectral musician is consistently described as a tall, young, white male wearing a vintage suit and tie. His fashion statement dates him as a revenant from the dance hall days.

Since the Theatre Project hosts a lot of traveling shows that feature pianists of their own, visiting performers have asked the Theatre Project staff the same question over and over throughout the years: "Who was that guy rehearsing in the lobby?"

The phantom piano player is partial to playing Schubert and seems to be activated when out-of-town musicians tickle the theater's ivories. Either his apparition appears or music emanates from other, seemingly unoccupied, rooms.

(Photo: Robbin Van Pelt)

Club Charles & Zodiac Restaurant – a haunted duplex.

CLUB CHARLES & ZODIAC RESTAURANT

Édouard André Neyt, a.k.a. "Frenchie," was born near Paris in 1925. During World War II, he served as double agent, feigning allegiance to the Germans while assisting the Allies.

After the war, he immigrated to Baltimore where he worked as a waiter and resided in an apartment at 1724 North Charles Street, above Club Charles.

The Frenchman died upstairs in 1979, supposedly from complications due to alcoholism. Although he was interred in a Prince George's County cemetery he seems to prefer his mortal digs. The ghost of the playful Frenchman puts in regular post-mortem appearances at the club. When witnessed his apparition is described as a "small, older gentleman in black trousers and white shirt," typical waiter wear.

The History Channel portrayed some of the waiter's antics when they showcased the club on *Haunted History - Baltimore*.

Liquor bottles, neatly arranged in rows at closing time, are often found jumbled up the next day. Staff have witnessed Frenchie's vaporous visage in the establishment's mirrors and patrons have seen a champagne glass fly off a shelf, hover in the air momentarily, then drop to the floor without breaking.

Frenchie's afterlife antics are as annoying as those he practiced when alive. After his shift ended, Frenchie would come to the club and harass the card players. He liked messing with their hair and trying to sit in their laps. To this day, some of the card players report that they feel him tousling their hair.

When Club Charles owner, Joy Martin, opened the Zodiac Restaurant next door to Club Charles she was flabbergasted that this place was also haunted - and not by a friendly ghost like Frenchie.

Also presented on the History Channel's popular *Haunted History* series, on occasion, a male apparition wearing an old-fashioned white linen suit waits for service at Table 3. Sometimes a small white dog accompanies him. When waiters approach the ghost, who appears as a flesh and blood patron, he dissipates right in front of their eyes.

A cook saw the unknown specter sitting with a drink in one hand and a cigarette in the other.

Those who have encountered the spirit say he exudes an evil aura. Employees complain that they often feel they're being watched and are filled with a sense of dread. A disembodied voice declaring, "Get out!" sent shivers down the spines of all those who heard it.

Sensitive souls make it a point to avoid the third-floor storage room. When the paranormal group, Ghost Hunters of Baltimore, visited the restaurant to investigate the site, one spirit seeker said an unseen hand tried to push her across the room and out the door.

Locals say that during Prohibition, the restaurant was a speakeasy run by a man named McKim. They allege that the former proprietor ended up hanging himself in the basement supposedly because his wife left him.

Could his death have been staged and was actually a murder?

Whatever the circumstance, the unabashed, bitter spirit stays behind, along with his neighbor Frenchie — a unique, post-mortem pair haunting Balto's nightspots.

OLD HUTZLERS

Hutzlers Department Store was once a highly regarded retail operation and innovative in that it was the first chain that did not discriminate against African-Americans.

In 1858, the Hutzlers Brothers established a dry goods store at the corner of Howard and Clay Streets. The business soon expanded into three small storefronts. In 1888, these stores were razed, and Hutzlers Palace was constructed on the site. Admired for it's Neo-Classical architecture the building remains one of Baltimore's landmarks.

The 1950's were its heyday - the downtown location flourished for over 30 years until an economic downturn forced Hutzlers to a new location in the Atrium building. Five years later Hutzler's Palace closed its doors for the last time.

Many reminisce about the old store and marvel over the festive spirit that haunted the place during the holidays when the sound of a ghostly bell echoed in the store. They surmise that the presence was a long-gone Santa, or Salvation Army worker, sharing its holiday spirit from beyond the grave.

BOLTON HILL ROWHOUSE

In the late 1980s residents living in the basement of a West Lafayette Street rowhouse experienced a series of unexplainable events.

At one time the basement apartment served as a women's outpatient clinic and was also the site of an annual rummage sale.

In one of the house's upper stories an owner claimed a death occurred on the premise when a gas refrigerator exploded in the early 1900s.

For whatever reason an uncomfortable presence was palpable in the apartment's atmosphere along with distinct cold spots – a certain sign of a ghostly presence.

Some other paranormal phenomena the inhabitants endured were small orbs of light swirling about the bedroom ceiling - the tiny comets even fascinated the cat; lights were found on when residents distinctly remembered turning them off.

One day as the tenant attempted to tidy up the storage room, she had a formidable experience. First, she had the uncomfortable feeling that she was being watched. Her apprehension became unbearable so she quickly headed for the door... it opened on its own!

As the woman sat for a while in the garden to regain her composure, a loud commotion and screeching sound emanated from the storeroom.

Struggling to open the stubborn door in order to investigate, she found that the trash she had put in garbage bags was thrown about; all her straightening had been for naught - the room was a mess again.

Surely the resident wraith felt its space had been invaded and was obviously ticked off.

Before the next tenant moved into the apartment he studied Ghost Extermination 101. His research prompted him to perform an ancient Asian exorcism ritual – he set fireworks off inside the house.

The pyrotechnics did the trick. Amazingly the haunting activity ceased.

BALTIMORE SCHOOL OF MASSAGE

In the still of the night when all is quiet at the Baltimore School of Massage, workers assert that long-ago voices pervade the space. Countless times when they go to investigate the noise the ghostly tones cease.

The school was erected at 6401 Dogwood Road on property that was once farmland. Little is known about the acreage except that the slaves who worked the land lived in structures that lined the low-lying area along the creek that runs behind the building.

When workmen were revamping the school, they had the eerie sensation that they were being watched; inexplicable banging in another part of the building sent shivers down their stalwart spines.

Ghost investigators from the Maryland Ghost & Spirit Association discovered high levels of electromagnetism indicating disturbances in the atmosphere. Their Infrared Thermal Scanners picked up temperature fluctuations and sharp decreases.[5] No surprise to the staffers who experience cold spots and feelings of unease.

The oddest manifestation of them all is the disembodied red scarf that floats down the long hallway.

---

[5] www.marylandghosts.com

This phenomenon has been witnessed by a handful of employees.

All accounts point to friendly spirits, but ghost hunters aren't happy when the unseen entities sap their camera batteries or cause their diagnostic equipment to go haywire.

The mysterious incidents only occur in certain sections of the building in conjunction with baffling power outages that exasperate employees.

Power drains usually accompany the presence of spirits – paranormal specialists assert that spirits need an energy source in order to manifest; this is a possible explanation for the power failures.

This writer feels the spirits hang around to enjoy the school's peaceful vibes and, as any recipient knows, a good massage feels heavenly. Perhaps the spirits hang around here because they feel as if they've already made it to the Other Side.

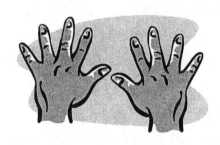

O'DONNELL HEIGHTS PHANTOM

The O'Donnell Heights phantom is one of Baltimore's most infamous spooks.

Established to house factory workers during the Second World War, O'Donnell Heights was a cohesive community and quite unique in that it was almost entirely surrounded by cemeteries.

In 1951, when the country was in the trenches of the Cold War, mass hysteria ensued when newspapers reported stories about an elusive prowler endowed with supernatural powers haunting the community.

The creature "had a hump on his back, and a horrible face."[b] He would lie in wait on rooftops and would leap down on unsuspecting victims; then he'd scurry off and disappear in nearby burial grounds.

In 19th century England a similar terror, termed "Spring-Heeled Jack," endowed with fiery eyes and the ability to spew blue-white flame from its mouth tormented London in 1838 by frightening females. The Aldershot military base was his target in 1870.

Baltimoreans alleged they saw the phantom easily leap over the barbed wire fences that bordered the burial

---

[b] Jesse Glass, "Spring-Heeled Jack's Violent Visits To Britain and the U.S."

grounds then it faded away among the headstones. At night, eerie organ music emanated from the cemetery chapel and was attributed to the specter.

Another mystifying aspect of the creature was that it never left footprints in the soft ground.

Hundreds of sightings were reported over a three-week period. Some of the interloper's charges were coaxing girls from underneath cars and burglarizing old ladies' homes.

Witnesses asserted that the specter wore a black cape and "walked like a drape and ran like a horse."[7]

Residents suffered many sleepless nights straining to hear the phantom track across their rooftops. Some took matters into their own hands and stood guard with rifles outside their houses, while others patrolled the neighborhood.

Not surprisingly, the phantasm was never apprehended. Many feel the O'Donnell Heights phantom was nothing but a cruel joke or simply a figment of over active imaginations. Whoever, or whatever, it was stirred a neighborhood into a frenzy at a time when tensions in our nation ran high.

---

[7] The *Baltimore Evening Sun.*

LOCUST POINT HOME

In the mid 19th century, Locust Point was much the same as it is now - a neighborhood of working class families. Around the time of the Civil War, however, a certain house located between Fort Avenue and Clement Street was considered haunted. The family that lived in the house believed that the spirit of the prior resident stayed behind.

The story goes that a poor family from England lived in the home. The woman had been brought up in an affluent family but had married "beneath" her. The couple and their two children immigrated to America hoping for a better life but making ends meet was a constant struggle.

The husband soon became ill and died leaving her to fend for herself and their young ones. Eventually she became destitute and was too proud to ask her family for assistance. Sadly, she was probably unaware that her neighbors would gladly have helped her if only she had known to ask.

Instead, they found her lifeless body in a rocking chair near a window. Her two small children lay dead in her lap. They had all starved to death.

Soon after the tragedy, neighbors began hearing strange noises coming from the home. Sometimes people caught sight of the Englishwoman's ghost seated at the window, rocking back and forth.

After that, any one who moved into the home didn't stay long - a negative energy pervaded the atmosphere. In 1865, residents claimed that a cold spot existed over a step on the staircase and no matter how many times they tried, when they attempted to carry an oil lamp or candle past this spot, the flame blew out.

The occupants heard crying throughout the house and an awful noise that sounded like a "Billy goat running over loose planks on a bridge." Given its history it was not surprising that they also reported the sound of a rocking chair creaking back and forth, even though they did not own one.

One of their children became very sick and was segregated in a ground floor room. One evening while the family was eating dinner, they heard the child scream. They ran to check on the boy who said that a lady had slapped him. Sure enough, the child had the distinct red imprint of a hand on his face. The family moved as soon as he recovered.

The Locust Point house still stands - happily inhabited by humans and free of fretful ghosts.

ACKNOWLEDGEMENTS

I want to especially thank Ms. Robbin Van Pelt, Professional Photographer & Photo Analyst, of Aberdeen, Maryland who assisted in my research and braved sub-zero weather (and challenging parking situations) to shoot photos for this book.

"Thank you" to the following individuals who provided stories and information:

Erin E. Collins, Marketing Manager,
Baltimore Museum of Industry
Jennifer Copeland & Francis O'Neil,
Maryland Historical Society
Russell J. Kujan, Membership Liaison,
Med Chi, The Maryland State Medical Society
Ellen von Karajan & Barbara Cromwell
The Preservation Society of Fell's Point
Ben Naas, Manager, Friends
Bill Oliver, Owner,
Wharf Rat Tavern

I also appreciate the stories shared by my other friends at Bertha's Mussels who choose to remain anonymous.

BIBLIOGRAPHY

Alexander, John, *GHOSTS, Washington's Most Famous Ghost Stories.* Washington Book Trading Company, Arlington, VA; 1988.

Alvarez, Rafael, "Oh, say, can you see ghosts at fort?" *Baltimore Sun*, Baltimore, MD; October 31, 1996.

Blackman, W. Haden, *The Field Guide to North American Hauntings.* Three Rivers Press, NY, NY; 1998.

Chalkley, Tom, Cohen, Charles, and Jensen, Brennen, "Baltimore's Ghost Stories to Tingle Your Spine." *Baltimore City Paper* Online; October 25 – 31, 2000. (www.citypaper.com).

Dunkle, Randy, "The Ghosts of Fells Point" (www.BaltimoreStories.com).

Glass, Jesse, "Spring-Heeled Jack's Violent Visits to Britain and the U.S." (www.rense.com)

Harman, Susan E., "Marcia C. Noyes: Making a Life." *Maryland Medical Journal;* April 1991.

Hauck, Dennis William, *National Directory of Haunted Places.* Penguin Books, New York, NY; 1996.

Holzer, Hans, *GHOSTS, True Encounters with the World Beyond.* Black Dog & Levanthal Publishers, New York, NY; 1998.

Jensen, Joseph E., "Med-Chi's Diligent Ghost." *Maryland Medical Journal;* March 1985.

_____ & Weisheit-Smith, Ingreet, "History of the Library of the Medical and Chirurgical Faculty of the State of Maryland." *Maryland State Medical Journal;* June 1980.

Kurluk, John, "Ghosts of Fells Point." *Ghost Trackers Newsletter,* Oak Lawn, IL; October 1987.

Mezensky, Catherine, "The Rocking Chair Ghost." (www.shadowlands.net)

Myers, Arthur, *The Ghostly Register.* Contemporary Books, Chicago, IL; 1986.

Olesker, Michael, "Bridge's reopening raises spirits along Charles Street." *Baltimore Sun*, Baltimore, MD.

Pitts, Jonathan, "The ghostly haunts of Fells Point leave one wanderer wondering, nothing more?" *Baltimore Sun*, Baltimore, MD; November 30, 2001.

Rukert, Norman, *Fort McHenry; Home of the Brave.* Bodine & Associates, Baltimore, MD; 1983.

Sellman, Jane, "Haunted Places in Baltimore." (www.lodging.com).

Williams, Rob, "Things That Go Bump in the Museum," *Volunteer News*, Baltimore Museum of Industry.

WEBSITES

The American Ghost Society: www.prairieghosts.com

B-More Ghosts: www.btco.net/ghosts

Edgar Allan Poe Society of Baltimore: www.eapoe.org

Francis Scott Key: www.usflag.org

Garrett-Jacobs Mansion: www.nps.gov

History of Fells Point: www.livebaltimore.com

John Hopkins University Gazette Online: www.jhu.edu

Leadbetters Tavern: www.leadbetterstavern.com

Maryland Ghost & Spirit Association: www.marylandghosts.com

Maryland's Online Community: www.sunspot.net

Maryland Paranormal Investigators Coalition: www.marylandparanormal.com

Preservation Society of Fells Point: www.preservationsociety.com

The Shadowlands: www.shadowlands.net

GHOST TOUR

(Photo: Robbin Van Pelt)

THE
PRESERVATION
SOCIETY'S

GHOSTWALK

Tours begin at the
Fell's Point
Visitor Center
808 S. Ann Street

For reservations:
410-675-6750

ABOUT THE PHOTOGRAPHER

...vard winning photographer Robbin Van Pelt is a lifelong Maryland ...ident and a graduate of the Visual Arts Program at Cecil ...mmunity College.

She is a board member for the Maryland Paranormal ...vestigator's Coalition (MD-PIC), a photographic analyst and ...vestigator for Greater Dundalk Paranormal Investigators (GDPI), ...d an investigator with the Baltimore Society of Paranormal ...earch (BSPR).

Ms. Van Pelt and the author met while joining with mutual ...ends on a ghost investigation at Gettysburg, Pennsylvania - one of ...erica's most haunted places.

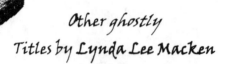

Other ghostly
Titles by Lynda Lee Macken

EMPIRE GHOSTS
New York State's Haunted Landmarks

GHOSTLY GOTHAM
New York City's Haunted History

ADIRONDACK GHOSTS ~ Volumes I & II

HAUNTED HISTORY OF STATEN ISLAND

HAUNTED SALEM & BEYOND

GHOSTS OF THE GARDEN STATE
Volumes I & II

HAUNTED CAPE MAY

BLACK CAT PRESS
Post Office Box 1218, Forked River, New Jersey 08731
E-mail: llmacken@hotmail.com